TEATIME AT GOLGOTHA

Mark Chrisler

I0141351

BROADWAY PLAY PUBLISHING INC
224 E 62nd St, NY, NY 10065
www.broadwayplaypub.com
info@broadwayplaypub.com

TEATIME AT GOLGOTHA
© Copyright 2014 by Mark Chrisler

First printing: June 2014
Second printing: February 2015
I S B N: 978-0-88145-600-4

Book design: Marie Donovan
Page make-up: Adobe InDesign
Typeface: Palatino
Printed and bound in the U S A

TEATIME AT GOLGOTHA was first staged at Prop
Thtr's National New Play Festival. It was produced
by Found Objects Theatre Group in conjunction with
Prop Thtr and The National New Play Network. It
opened 6 July 2007 at The Prop Thtr in Chicago with
the following cast and creative contributors:

LONGINUS.. Matt Glaz
QUINTUS... David Bettino
CABRAL.. Jonathan Whitted
JOHANNES KEPLER...Tim Racine
TYCHO BRAHE...Joel Stanley Huff
JEBB ....Pete Blatchford
MICHAEL .... Lyle Fredericks
IANTHE ....Nicole Richwalsky
NICHOLAS... Andrew Schoen

Director..Kevlyn Hayes
Set design ....Emily Altman
Technical direction...Sean Walters

CHARACTERS & SETTING:

LONGINUS, *a Roman soldier who stabbed Jesus on the cross to ensure his death*
QUINTUS, *a Roman general who pioneered the phrase "women, can't live with 'em, can't live without 'em"*
CABRAL, *a Roman soldier*
JOHANNES KEPLER, *a German astronomer*
TYCHO BRAHE, *a Scanian astronomer and nobleman*
JEBB, *a clairvoyant dwarf, court jester and servant to* TYCHO
MICHAEL, *a young sculptor of action figures*
IANTHE, *a poet and the girlfriend of* MICHAEL
NICHOLAS, *squatter at the apartment of* MICHAEL

Location:
The Hill of Golgotha, immediately following the crucifixion
TYCHO's banquet hall, immediately following a large party
MICHAEL's bedroom, modernity

ACT ONE

(At open, three playing areas are apparent, although two are black. The third shows two more-or-less Roman soldiers, waiting for a third.)

CABRAL: How are his eyes?

QUINTUS: Yes, I've heard those stories.

CABRAL: And?

QUINTUS: Either he's blind or he's not, isn't that the way?

(LONGINUS enters, he carries a spear.)

CABRAL: Hail, Longinus of Gaius Cassius!

LONGINUS: Hail, friend Cabral.

QUINTUS: Hail, Longinus!

LONGINUS: Hail, Quintus Caecilius Metellus Macedonicus.

CABRAL: Is that your new pilum, Longinus?

QUINTUS: A new pilum? What's this?

LONGINUS: Yes, I have purchased a new pilum, as the old was naught but a pile of splinters held together solely by the will of Mars.

QUINTUS: Well, do proffer it here.

CABRAL: Need I remind you that there remain lots to be drawn?

QUINTUS: Lots can wait, Longinus has a new pilum!

CABRAL: I know it.

QUINTUS: Come, show your new pilum.

LONGINUS: *(Passing the spear to* QUINTUS*)* It took me quite the while to hoard the necessary funds. As you can see, it's a vast improvement over the standard issue. The hilt…

QUINTUS: Why is it wet?

LONGINUS: Hm? No, that's blood.

CABRAL: Blood, eh? And what would blood be doing on your new pilum?

LONGINUS: What mean you? Blood is the most appropriate adornment for a pilum, new or old.

QUINTUS: *(Smelling his hands)* What sort of blood is this?

LONGINUS: I don't know…Jew?

QUINTUS: It's more like…water.

CABRAL: Humble Longinus, washing his spear.

QUINTUS: So, what do we have here?

LONGINUS: Hm? There? Up there? Thief, messiah, thief.

CABRAL: I'd think a Jew's blood would be thicker and blacker than Roman blood, not thin and clear.

QUINTUS: So many messiahs. So many thieves, too…

LONGINUS: Of course.

QUINTUS: But SOOO many messiahs.

CABRAL: Less than thieves.

LONGINUS: But thieves are to be expected.

QUINTUS: Yes, to some extent, thieves are a sign of a healthy country.

LONGINUS: Like fleas on a strong, fat dog.

QUINTUS: But messiahs? Who's ever heard of such a thing?

LONGINUS: More like ticks, I'd say.

QUINTUS: What's that?

LONGINUS: More like ticks. On a dog, I mean.

QUINTUS: …Elaborate.

CABRAL: He says that messiahs are like ticks on a dog, if, that is to say, thieves are fleas.

QUINTUS: Yes, I…but how so?

LONGINUS: Ticks, like fleas, live on a healthy beast.

QUINTUS: Certainly.

LONGINUS: But, you see, with fleas you might measure the health of the dog to be good, or else, it: stands to reason, the fleas would leave.

CABRAL: Of course.

LONGINUS: But ticks, while they may present the illusion of health—if we think of them as indicators such that fleas are—can spread their pestilence. They drink, and once they've started to drinking their thirst is only sated when they are bloated and stupid. Meanwhile, the dog, which on the outside seems healthy, bleeds blood that is vile and thin. Blood that is…

CABRAL: Like water?

QUINTUS: Like water. *(Silence)* To the lots, then?

LONGINUS: To the lots.

(Blackout on The Romans. Lights up on a large banquet table. Goblets and food stuff are cast about, as at the end of a raucous party that has gone on who knows how long. TYCHO BRAHE sits at the table, drunk and in ill health. He is a large man, a glutton, and he has a golden nose which serves as a replacement for that which was lopped off in a

duel long ago. Underneath the table sits JEBB, *a dwarf who acts both as* TYCHO's *personal servant and court jester.)*

JEBB: What has he done to earn them, though? He doesn't do the work, he doesn't make the sacrifices. He just waits to take them from you.

TYCHO: No: it's his eyes. He'd do it himself if he could. He loves the stars as much as I do. Maybe more, if he's been willing to stay, knowing I won't give them to him.

JEBB: You give him too much credit. Especially considering…

*(*JOHANNES KEPLER *enters.)*

KEPLER: You called?

TYCHO: You know that our disagreements have nothing to do with some silly religious scribbling?

KEPLER: Has everyone left?

TYCHO: I'd be inclined to believe you, Earth round the Sun and the rest of it, except for the parallax, you know.

KEPLER: Are you alright?

JEBB: Mister Brahe is quite fine and has requested your company so that the two of you might…

KEPLER: Yes, Jebb, I'm quite aware.

TYCHO: You know that, right?

KEPLER: Has he been drinking?

TYCHO: Kepler! You know that, right?

KEPLER: Certainly, Tycho.

TYCHO: I'm no nitwit without a nova, you know?

KEPLER: Of course. Whatever you say. He looks ill.

JEBB: Mister Brahe is quite fine and has requested your company so that the two of you might…

KEPLER: You've made all of this abundantly clear. Tycho, I know full well the nature of your beliefs and do not count you amongst that particular brand of rabble. The rabble that makes its God of a chemical blindness, however, I find you quite suited to.

TYCHO: Drinking? Drinking, you mean? Do you know why I wear this golden nose?

KEPLER: May I assume it's because of some combination of drunken foolishness and gluttonous vanity?

TYCHO: Yes! You may very well do that.

KEPLER: Then yes; I know.

TYCHO: You MAY assume that. But you'd be wrong.

KEPLER: That right?

TYCHO: Yes, well, largely you'd be right, sure.

KEPLER: Great. Then, is that all?

TYCHO: Yes, yes… No! Come, sit with me. Drink.

KEPLER: You know I don't. And I know you shouldn't.

TYCHO: Not that sort of drink, Kepler: tea. Jebb! Bring the tea!

JEBB: Yes, my lord. *(He scurries off stage.)*

KEPLER: My Lord?

TYCHO: You watch your mouth, huh? That little dwarf knows more than you and I can dream…. Dream? Dream? Jebb!

JEBB: *(Off stage)* Readying the tea, my Lord!

TYCHO: He'll just be a minute… He's readying the tea.

KEPLER: Uh-huh.

TYCHO: He has something very important to tell you for me.

KEPLER: Then he can deliver his message along with my tea, in my room.

TYCHO: You're going to want to stay.

KEPLER: It would take a lot for me to want that.

TYCHO: I know exactly what it would take, and I'm saying: you're going to want to stay.

(*Blackout on* KEPLER *and* TYCHO. *Lights up on the third scene: a small bedroom.* IANTHE *and* MICHAEL *are arguing. She stands pacing, throwing clothes and the like in a bag. He sits on the bed.*)

IANTHE: You just don't see it.

(*There is a knock at the door.*)

MICHAEL: So tell me. What can I do? What can I say? I'll do it. I'll say it.

(*Another knock*)

IANTHE: What can you do to get what you want. That's it all over, Michael.

MICHAEL: Please. Just stay.

(*Another, louder knock. This time noticed*)

IANTHE: What now?

(NICHOLAS *begins opening the door.*)

NICHOLAS: Hey, Mike? Hey? Mike? Mike, you up?

IANTHE: Michael?

MICHAEL: Hmm?

NICHOLAS: Mike, I've got something important to tell you.

MICHAEL: What?

NICHOLAS: I've got something to tell you.

MICHAEL: Can't it wait?

NICHOLAS: It's pretty important.

IANTHE: What is it, Nick?

NICHOLAS: Oh, hi Ianthe… Sorry. Sorry to wake you, I mean.

IANTHE: What's going on?

NICHOLAS: There's something I have to tell Michael.

MICHAEL: Fine, so tell me.

NICHOLAS: *(Picking up an action figure near* MICHAEL's *bed)* Is this the new one you're working on?

MICHAEL: Hmmm? Yeah, yeah. What's going on, Nick?

NICHOLAS: What is he?

MICHAEL: He's, um, the god of war.

NICHOLAS: Mars?

MICHAEL: Yeah, sure.

IANTHE: Nicholas, we're bu…trying to sleep.

NICHOLAS: I bet you are. Huh?

IANTHE: What?

NICHOLAS: You know…

IANTHE: Okay, you can talk in the morning…

NICHOLAS: No, I need to talk to him now.

IANTHE: Then you can go in the other room. I need to sleep.

NICHOLAS: No. No one's leaving this room.

IANTHE: What?

MICHAEL: Fine. Stay or go…crawl into fucking bed for all I care, but I'm trying to sleep.

IANTHE: What do you mean, Nicholas?

NICHOLAS: I know you are, I know. I'm sorry. I'm just trying to talk to you.

IANTHE: Then just say what you have to say already.

NICHOLAS: See, that's the thing. I don't know how to say it.

MICHAEL: Words usually work. Take a verb, a noun or two…string'em together. That sorta shit.

NICHOLAS: …I think I may have made a mistake…

IANTHE: Nick, you're freaking me out.

NICHOLAS: I'm sorry. I'm really sorry.

IANTHE: That's okay; just tell us what's going on.

NICHOLAS: No, not that. I'm sorry, Michael.

MICHAEL: You're forgiven. Go to bed.

IANTHE: Have you been drinking?

NICHOLAS: I think I killed your dog.

MICHAEL: What?

(Blackout on the bedroom. Lights up on KEPLER *and* TYCHO.*)*

TYCHO: Rix is dead.

KEPLER: And Rix is?

TYCHO: My elk. My elk drank himself to death.

KEPLER: Oh. I'm…so…sorry.

TYCHO: Who would've thought he could? He was an elk, you know? Pretty big. He must have drunk a helluva lot.

KEPLER: Are you sure?

TYCHO: I know a dead elk when I see one. Only man you'll ever know owned an elk. Only one. I loved that thing.

KEPLER: And…that's why you called me here?

TYCHO: No, no. That's just…filling time.

KEPLER: Good.

TYCHO: Camaraderie maybe, if you'd owned an elk.

KEPLER: Because I was hoping we were here to talk about your charts.

TYCHO: But you haven't. Or, not to my knowledge. Who am I kidding…

JEBB: *(Entering with teapot, cups and saucers)* The tea has been readied!

TYCHO: Tea now! Kepler, have some tea.

KEPLER: Just tea?

JEBB: Just tea.

KEPLER: Alright.

(There is a moment of silence while they drink their tea.)

TYCHO: Jebb has something important to tell you.

KEPLER: That so?

TYCHO: Yes. Jebb has something important to tell you for me. *(He doubles over in pain)*

KEPLER: Are you sure you're alright?

TYCHO: I've had a dream. Jebb, proclaim my dream!

JEBB: The proclamation!

(Blackout on TYCHO, *et al, lights up on* LONGINUS*)*

A VOICE: *Eloi, eloi: lama sabachthani?!*

QUINTUS: Someone make favor and close his mouth.

LONGINUS: *(Looking over his shoulder)* I think that was pretty much it.

QUINTUS: Good then.

CABRAL: Would that just one of these mongrels could be crucified with a bit of dignity.

LONGINUS: Not to be contrary, but it's possible that the act of being crucified rules that option out.

CABRAL: Still…

QUINTUS: Somebody's awfully cynical today.

LONGINUS: Me? No. Not practically, at least. Maybe the philosophical end…I don't know.

QUINTUS: Dangerous talk.

LONGINUS: Psht! Barely talk at all.

CABRAL: What do you mean, "the philosophical end"?

(Lights immediately go to black on The Romans and go up on MICHAEL, etc. He is standing, angrily NICHOLAS is fearful, a subservient pose.)

MICHAEL: What the fuck you mean, "killed my dog"?

NICHOLAS: I regret it.

MICHAEL: Fuck right you do! Where is he?

NICHOLAS: The living room. The corner… Rat poison.

MICHAEL: Holy shit, Nick, I'm gonna fuck you up something fierce.

(MICHAEL runs toward the doorway, to get past NICHOLAS.)

NICHOLAS: No. No going out that door. *(Pulling a gun from his pocket)*

MICHAEL: Good fucking…

IANTHE: What's that?

MICHAEL: It's a fucking gun.

IANTHE: Obviously it's a fucking gun, Michael. What the hell is he doing with it?

MICHAEL: Well I don't know now, do I…?

NICHOLAS: Sssshhhut up! I'm going to explain myself. I'm going to explain and you're going to listen. I need you to sit down.

(MICHAEL does not.)

IANTHE: This is just some kind of dream.

(Lights down on bedroom scene. Lights up on the banquet)

JEBB: A dream in three parts! Lord Brahe, not having slept properly in a number of days, has taken to dictating the segments presented to him. In the midst of the great and last banquet…

KEPLER: Last?

JEBB: Amongst the reveling, which was of a scale and opulence to which the friends of Lord Brahe are acquainted, he slept three times. Such was his hospitality that even during these brief respites he remained at the table and whispered intermittently in my ear.

(Lights down on the banquet, up on The Romans)

LONGINUS: I dare not speak about it in tone greater than a whisper.

QUINTUS: Come now, we're all friends.

CABRAL: And what is a secret between friends?

LONGINUS: Less and less a secret, I should think.

QUINTUS: Lack of trust… disheartens me. I've always found that.

CABRAL: Lots, then?

QUINTUS: I swear, Cabral, you're worse than that one with all his "My God, My God" garbage. Go ahead, good Longinus.

LONGINUS: I was thinking, just today—and just thinking—about what an odd thing it is; death. Or acclimation to death. An odd thing, too, being a soldier. Different than, say, an accountant. But not as different as you'd imagine. Which is the weird part. Because it only makes sense that accounting would become routine. Yawning at your abacus is not perturbing

in the way that is yawning at your spear. Everyday:
form phalanx, thrust, stab, assure the dead their state,
eviscerate the crucified…it doesn't speak well to the
health of one's humors to enter these emptily. I've been
thinking these things…ruminating—not just today,
for a while—and it came to me that perhaps I might
alter my routine, as to lend it novelty. For instance,
there is a rhythm, a rather sing-songy pace at which
I tend to conduct my exercises and killings. So one
day I tried altering it, altering the song by which I
choreographed my murders. Where I had sung "to kill
is but a soldier's job and living for the wives," I now
sung "what justice is there but for the spear and peace
by candle and fat." But it soon occurred to me that this
was merely a change in distractionary tactics, and not
that great of one, at that. Things still seemed…blurry.
No. Not blurry, but…shaky. As if the world and I
were moving, but it was moving slower and without
direction. Or maybe that was me wandering sidestep.
Perhaps my impression that it was the world was just
a…failure of imagination. In any event, next I turned
to contemplation and prayer, which seemed sage and
perhaps could have been, save that I never had felt
much religious fervor, so, frankly, the whole thing felt
put-on and platitudinous. It was at this time I started
saving for a new pilum, thinking that, if nothing else,
it would keep me keen by its alien balance and weight.
In the meantime I tried on a plethora of idiosyncratic
behaviors: spitting and women's undergarments and
drink—plenty of drink—all paramount failures in their
own rights; until today, when I received this pilum. It
goes without saying that I was very excited and went
about my duties gleefully. Things were different, if
only in feel, but within an hour the weightless mail
of routine had once again enveloped me. Such is the
nature of this beast that almost immediately after
noticing, it fled my mind and left me with my "to kill

is but a soldier's job and living for the wives." It was
on that beat that I thrust my spear into the Nazarene's
side and was struck by a deluge of water. That did
it. Shocked me the way nothing had. Song or prayer
or the new spear. I looked up and saw death…really
saw it. Then, slowly, I lowered my head and saw it
everywhere. That water woke me fiercely. I saw all I
had ever done and it was terrible, but precisely what I
needed. This ambivalence, too, was odd. And then, just
now as I approached, I thought of the accountant and
wondered what he would do if his abacus broke in the
middle of his calculations. And then I thought "that
would be completely different, because he would no
longer be able to do his job." Although, now I wonder
if that would be different at all.

(Blackout on The Romans, lights up on the banquet)

JEBB: The dream, part one! Mister Brahe, while casually
walking down a fine island road, unexpectedly came
upon the house of his childhood, which was peculiar
for a number of reasons, as, for one, he had thought
himself nowhere near this home as he walked. In
addition, the house was much smaller and, dare I say,
homelier—not homier, but homelier, you see—than
he remembered. Curious, he entered the home to find
yet another surprise: however more humble the facade
of his boyhood dwelling had seemed, the inside had
grown twenty times in grandeur. There were many
rooms, moving as if by clockwork, rotating both on
an axis and around the center, which was stationary,
but rather than being inconvenient, he found he
always seemed to get where he wanted to, despite his
disorientation. He decided to see what was in the large,
middle room and started heading in what he figured
would be the correct direction. When he reached the
middle, whom did he find but his boyhood love, now

fully grown, and the man who had graciously granted
him his golden nose after a well-fought duel.

(JEBB *looks back for approval of this description from* TYCHO,
who grants it. Satisfied, he continues:)

JEBB: They and a small number of others, whom Mister
Brahe could not exactly place, seemed to be setting
up a play, a work of theatre, and were doing so in a
hurried—yet professional—manner. He came forward
to greet them but was rebuked, curtly. This made him
feel very uncomfortable with these people from his
youth, and he made a speedy egress through a large set
of double-doors. He found himself in a spiral stairway
which he ascended to the house's next level. He
opened another set of doors and found himself again in
this center room. Looking around now, he noticed that
it was far greater in size than had been all the other
spinning rooms combined and tall beyond description.
Seated, all around, on levels high above and far below,
were masses of audience, assembled, no doubt, for the
aforementioned play. The play quickly swung into
motion, a courtroom drama, he realized, although he
was not sure who was on trial, or, indeed, for what.
He kneeled behind the lip of the balcony to take a
better look around: the whole room was now dressed
in streamers and banners of incredible fabric and size.
He could hear the actors speaking, but could not locate
them amidst the various viewing areas and garnish.
Suddenly, it seemed that the voices of the actors had
become significantly louder, and he turned around to
find he was on the playing area of the stage. He ducked
behind the lip in order not to obfuscate the audience's
view and draw attention to himself, but his young
love was already hissing vitriol at him and ordering
him to leave. Now, this being Lord Brahe's home, he
was hesitant to comply with such uncouthly phrased
demands, but he also has a healthy respect for the arts,

and so he crawled out the entrance on his belly. Back
in the stairway he began to climb and climb, passing
door after door and feeling very upset about the whole
situation.

After what seemed like hours—although I can attest
to this entire incident occurring within but a few
waking minutes—he reached the roof, which, as he
looked out over the top, he saw to be no more than
eight feet from the ground. He leaned over the edge
and a cat jumped over his back and landed on the
ground below. Following this, a veritable cornucopia
of animals came bounding out of a window just under
his head and through cracks and holes in the walls and
foundation. Some were mice and rats, but there were
also miniature pack animals, a bison carrying much
cargo even, though it was no larger than six inches tall.
Brahe figure the terror behind this diaspora augured
terrible cataclysm for him if he were to remain upon
the roof. And so, with bravery and gumption, Mister
Brahe threw himself from the roof and was caught on
the backs of a family of raccoons, who broke his fall
and carried him briskly away, never to catch even a
glance of his old house, or its fate, again. (*A moment of
silence*) END DREAM ONE!

(*Lights out on the banquet, up on the bedroom*)

NICHOLAS: This has to do with you, too, Ianthe.
Although ideally I'd tell you separately. See, the thing
is that I loved you from the time I met you. God.
And, I'll tell you, at first I think you loved me, too.
It's not that I thought you loved me, I think you did,
honestly…but I'm not asking for you to tell me. You
might not remember, really. (*Spotting* IANTHE's *bag*)
What good did you think that would do? Ha! But when
we first met you and I were really, like, huggy, right?
And you weren't that way with everyone. Huggier
than most, yeah, but not with everyone. And, it's like,

I thought there was romance blooming, blossoming,
whatever…starting there. Except then we started
kissing—not romantically—just like, these friendly
little kisses, and it was just…I knew it was over. I
mean our chance. I thought about it and tried to figure
out how one time, maybe, when we kissed like that, I
might be able to hold it out, to make it a real kiss. But
you'd have to figure out you loved me, which I really
feel you would have, before you were shocked at what
I was doing, you know? And that shock would come
real quick, I knew that. It's not that I'm judging you, I
mean that shock would come quick for anyone. And
then the two of you started getting close, or, I guess,
different, so…it just seemed like "what the hell," you
know, `cause on some level you both knew about me,
me standing there while you cuddled up and…fuck!
And Michael, Mike, geez, you know? I mean, I don't
get it. We've been friends so long and it—I'm sorry—
but it's fucking ridiculous all this luck you get. You
go to like, what, two semesters at Ohio, drop out and
end up with this sweet job…I mean, sculpting action
figures? What the fuck? And I slave away at Brandeis,
get this English degree and I'm squatting on your
fucking couch? Did you know that, Ianthe? I have a
degree in English from Brandeis. Hell of a school to do
that, I don't have to tell you. And you end up doing
the dude making Mars for Mattel. He doesn't—I'd
be able to appreciate your poetry so much more than
him. I do, actually. But I'd help, giving you these little
critiques, and everyone of them, I'd kiss you, those
little pecks like we used to, so that you'd know I was
trying to improve you and that I loved you. And I'd
buy you a manual typewriter and we'd have a little
sun room where you'd type in the morning, crawling
out of bed and draping a sheet over your body, and I'd
pretend to be asleep and listen to you type, just listen
to the rhythm of your fingers, until you came in with

tea to wake me, and we'd just be so sweet like that, you
know? But I listen, or hear, I guess. I hear you guys,
but I don't want to listen. I hear you talking and I hear
you…just all the time. And it doesn't seem fair. But
no big deal, right? That's breaks. Sure, sure. Except
last night, I was feeling sick. I got up and I heard you
talking…I was right outside your door, just crouched
there listening, not trying to listen, I mean, but
listening, just accidentally, seriously. And I heard you.
I heard you talking and I couldn't believe it. Talking
and laughing and plotting. So, after you were done, I
made sure you couldn't do what you said you were
going to do, and I thought, that's it: no harm, no foul.
But the more I rested on it…ruminated on it, the more I
thought that's it, that's the straw. Things had just gone
too far and I needed to balance them. But I didn't want
to hurt you. Hurt you like you were going to hurt me,
because you hadn't—haven't, yet—but like you had
hurt me in the past. So…the dog.

IANTHE: Nicholas…

NICHOLAS: Shut up! Everyone be quiet for a minute.

*(Lights go down on the bedroom and come up on the
banquet, where JEBB is catching his breath while the others
watch him.)*

(There is the sound of an elk, walking offstage.)

*(Lights go down on the banquet and come up on The
Romans, with CABRAL and QUINTUS staring awkwardly at
LONGINUS.)*

*(Lights go down on The Romans and back up on the
bedroom.)*

NICHOLAS: I put some rat poison in with his food, and
he bounded up to eat it like you don't even feed him,
Mike. It didn't seem like it hurt him much, which was
good, 'cause I didn't even hate the dog. Liked him

a lot, really. And I wish I hadn't done it, 'cause now
it seems so silly. I mean, I think you two still need
to be punished a lot more, and that makes the dog
kind of, you know, superfluous. He ate so much. Just
something to see, eating so much.

(Lights out on the bedroom, lights up on the banquet)

JEBB: The dream, part two:

(Lights out on the banquet, cutting JEBB *off. Lights up on
The Romans)*

QUINTUS: Um… To the lots then?

LONGINUS: Yes, sure.

CABRAL: Finally.

(Lights out on the Romans, lights up on the banquet)

JEBB: The dream, part two:

(Lights down on the banquet, lights up on the bedroom)

MICHAEL: *(Calmly, as to disarm the situation)* Nick,
buddy, I don't know what you're talking about. I'm
sorry if you had feelings for Ianthe, but all this…
whatever it is, it's in your head.

NICHOLAS: *(Raising the gun at* MICHAEL*)* Shut up!
You're no good, Mike. You're no good at all. And
you're a liar and you're not even good at that. I don't
know how you found out about it, but it's not for you.

MICHAEL: Nick…

NICHOLAS: Sit down!

MICHAEL: *(Backing up and sitting on the bed)* Okay, I'm
sitting down, alright? Just cool off.

NICHOLAS: No good. No good. But, I'm gonna be
better. We're gonna have a trial, huh? I've always
thought…have you ever read Hobbes? *The Leviathan*?
No? Of course not. Ianthe, you've read Thomas
Hobbes, right? See! There's another thing! Don't let

me get off track. Hobbes got me thinking a lot about capitol punishment, if it's moral or not, you see. And I'm not sure if it serves a greater good, but that really isn't the issue, the way I see Hobbes. It's more about the terms of the contract—social contract. The thing is, in Hobbes day, death wasn't—being sentenced to death, I mean—wasn't the worst punishment. Banishment. You know, exile? Even up when Shakespeare wrote, right Ianthe? Juliet says something about banishment being worse than death? Anyway, so morally, I think we've got the right to it—execution, not exile, we can obviously morally exile people, even though we don't anymore, so maybe not—I think, except for some little problems, and one of those is innocence. If someone is innocent but convicted, and we kill then, well, then, no one is safe. I'm not sure a state can ever know, I mean really know that a person is guilty, know well enough to kill them. But I can. I can know that. About the two of you. And don't worry! We're talking about something safer here. But worse, I think. Like in Hobbes' day. Not even entering the suicide element. And I think I know…goes without saying, right? But I'm willing to entertain arguments. Willing to hear the story.

(*Lights down on the bedroom, lights up on the banquet*)

JEBB: The dream, part two:

(*Lights down on the banquet, lights up on the bedroom*)

IANTHE: Shut up! Shut up, you fucking lunatic! On trial for what, you fucking loony toon?! Michael…

NICHOLAS: Ianthe, I don't want you to be upset.

IANTHE: Stay away from me.

NICHOLAS: No, no. I don't want you to be scared of me.

IANTHE: You don't…you fucking nutjub! What the hell's gone wrong with you?

(NICHOLAS *approaches* IANTHE. *He kneels on the bed,*
moving towards her. As he crosses, MICHAEL *makes a lunge*
for the gun. They struggle briefly and NICHOLAS *smacks*
MICHAEL *with the hilt of the pistol, knocking him to the bed.*
Lights out on the bedroom, up on the banquet.)

JEBB: The dream, part two: (*He waits a second, looking*
around as if to make sure the lights won't go down again)
The dream, part two: After waking and facilitating
the initial dream to me, Tycho Brahe made a valiant
display of festiveness before falling for a second nap.
It is quite likely that the second dream was totally
separate from the first, as much as things can be
separate, dreams in particular, but for the sake of
continuity, let us say that the family of raccoons carried
him all the way to the ocean and that then, in an act of
aquatic derring-do far greater than ever would have
been expected from such animals, they ferried him to
a lush island where upon sat two buildings, each with
one occupant, both of whom welcomed him graciously
and shared both their friendship and board, namely a
garden of artichokes which comprised a near totality of
their diet, especially once the raccoons—bless them—
ran out. These island men were preyed upon by an
illness, or maybe two distinct yet similar illnesses, that
rendered their recollection faulty. One of them, short
and squat, had a memory that gave way every day, so
that each morning was fresh and unburdened by the
morning before. Every waking brought itself upon a
blank slate. The other man, taller and more wiry, had
a similar predicament, save that his memory lasted
for two days, though towards the end of the second
the beginning of the first became vague and riddled
with errors. Neither of them used the buildings at all,
instead sleeping out on the sand and under the stars.
Neither one of them remembered ever seeing a cloudy
sky, let alone a squall, which, obviously given their

amnesia didn't mean a whole lot, but on with it. After a
week with them, Mister Brahe suddenly had a striking
portend: he came upon the knowledge that a storm
would be coming in exactly seven days and that the
three needed to make preparations. Artichokes had to
be harvested and salted for preservation, the shelters
needed reinforcement from long disuse. The two men
began to fight in this process, which slowed the work
considerably, and right before the storm they reached
a boiling point and retired to separate quarters. The
man with two days' memory would remind the squat
man of their quarrel every other day, and then, having
forgotten himself, would go about business as usual,
until, frustrated again, the cycle would renew. Mister
Brahe was forced to make a choice and, considering
that the taller man was slightly closer to him in mind-
set, he bunked with him. The storm came and sat upon
them, blowing and bellowing for days. Every day the
two men would shout back and forth at each other
over the roaring thunder, sometimes to tell them how
they hated one another and other times to remind them
why. When the noise of the storm was too great to even
yell across, the tall man would begrudgingly address
our master, but usually only to run by him his fantasies
of poisoning the squat man. This annoyed Mister
Brahe. The tall man was so pompous about his mental
faculties that it was all he talked about, bragging about
his incredible memory, "at least two hundred percent
better than his," he would shout, "maybe more, but
who remembers?" It drove our poor master up a
wall. He shouted, one day, to the squat man that he
wished he had taken residence with him, not fearing
to offend the tall man as he would only forget in two
days anyhow…although why it was worth telling
the man who would forget even sooner, who knows?
Commiseration, I suppose. He put to mind that he
would move over to the other mans' cabin and, the

next day, set out in the storm. He was merely ten paces or so from the squat man's abode when a roaring water spout came and ripped him from the earth, and at that, he awoke again. *(A moment of silence)* END DREAM TWO!

(Lights down on the banquet, up on The Romans, drawing lots. After a moment:)

QUINTUS: You know, I heard somewhere recently, that desertion is the worst crime a man can commit. Just, you know, apropos of nothing. I thought I'd say. *(A moment)* Have you heard that, Longinus?

CABRAL: What about murder?

QUINTUS: Murder has the worse punishment, but desertion is the worse crime.

CABRAL: Why would they give the lesser crime a greater punishment.

QUINTUS: Well, you see, the punishment for murder is exile.

CABRAL: Uh huh.

QUINTUS: But you can't exile a deserter, can you?

CABRAL: Why not?

QUINTUS: Because it sort of sends the wrong message, don't you think?

CABRAL: How?

QUINTUS: Your punishment for wanting to leave is to be forced to leave?

CABRAL: Ah. Yes. That is a conundrum.

QUINTUS: Yes. A conundrum. So, to avoid a tautology—or something like that—we must be content to punish deserters with out penultimate sentence.

CABRAL: Which is?

QUINTUS: Death.

CABRAL: Hey! That's sort of funny: murderers leave and leavers are murdered.

QUINTUS: Yes. Executed. Did you know that, Longinus?

LONGINUS: Yes.

QUINTUS: Like common thieves.

LONGINUS: Common messiahs.

(There is a long silence.)

CABRAL: All that water came from one guy, huh?

LONGINUS: Hm? Uh, yes. I suppose.

CABRAL: Must've drunk a helluva lot.

LONGINUS: I guess so.

(Silence)

CABRAL: Or you hit his water bladder.

(Silence)

QUINTUS: His what?

CABRAL: What's that?

QUINTUS: Hit his water bladder?

CABRAL: Yes. All the desert peoples have them. Like camels.

(Silence)

LONGINUS: They don't, you know.

CABRAL: How's that?

QUINTUS: Water bladders. They don't have them.

LONGINUS: I'm not sure about camels, either.

CABRAL: Well, agree to disagree.

(Silence)

QUINTUS: I'm sorry…no. No "agree to disagree."
One agrees to disagree, if one does—and usually I do
not—if the subject at hand is a matter of opinion or
metaphysics.

CABRAL: So?

QUINTUS: So, one can clearly find a formal, definitive
answer as to the existence of water bladders, and that
answer, clearly, is in the contra.

LONGINUS: I can't take anymore of this.

QUINTUS: You see: you've upset Longinus.

CABRAL: Longinus was upset far before me, what with
the…

LONGINUS: I say, I can't take anymore of this.

QUINTUS: Alright. Let's everyone quiet down. Silence
makes good friendships.

(Silence)

QUINTUS: Silence makes good friendships…not a
popular adage, but it has its merits, I think.

(Silence)

LONGINUS: I can't take anymore of this.

CABRAL: Aye, me!

QUINTUS: Silence that insipid maw of yours, Cabral.
Now, Longinus, I understand tedium. Tell me, do I
understand tedium?

CABRAL: He does.

QUINTUS: I'll say it again, Cabral! I do, I do. I
understand it all too well. Painful stuff it can be. Sure.
But, good Longinus…that is, I'm a friend of debate.
Healthy debate. Why, just a few weeks ago a few of
the local officers and I were discussing the efficiency
of different knife sharpening techniques. And did it
get heated? Yes, I'll say so. That's half the fun. But

in the end all went back to as it had been. I, by the
way, prefer counter-clockwise swipes of the stone,
starting at the hilt and moving up towards the edge.
Traditional, sure: but effective. That's my point, you
see. All this…pontification I accept it. I encourage it.
But when the sun sets on these thoughts they are to
retire, not to drag across the horizons as if tethered to
it. So I'll have no more of this "can't take this" talk, you
see.

(Lights up on the bedroom)

IANTHE: I can't take anymore of this.

(Lights down on the bedroom)

QUINTUS: Now, you see, that's exactly what I'm talking
about. We all have things we don't want to do. I
don't necessarily enjoy seeing my wife sometimes as
frequently as twice a month, but I do it anyway. For
the good of the state. And if you think you can shirk
your responsibilities, I've a word or two for you, yes.

(Lights down on The Romans, up on the dining room)

JEBB: The dream, part three!

KEPLER: I can't take anymore of this.

TYCHO: Excuse me?

KEPLER: How long is this going to go on? If we're
coming to a point here, please let us hurry it up.

(Lights down on the dining room, up on the bedroom)

IANTHE: What's the point of all this? If you know we're
"guilty"? And Michael…

NICHOLAS: I want this to be painless.

(Lights up on the dining room)

TYCHO: I'm sorry, what?

(Lights down on the dining room)

NICHOLAS: It's really only partly my idea. A lot of it comes from… you know, him. A mandate, really.

(Lights down on the bedroom, up on The Romans)

LONGINUS: What do you mean by that?

QUINTUS: I hear more than you say, Longinus.

(Lights up on the dining room)

KEPLER: Can you not hear me?

(Lights down on the dining room)

QUINTUS: There's dissent in your voice.

CABRAL: You signed the contract.

(Lights up on the bedroom down on The Romans)

NICHOLAS: You broke the rules.

(Lights down on the bedroom, up on the dining room)

TYCHO: I allow you into my home, and you haven't the respect to honor my wishes?

KEPLER: What wishes?

TYCHO: To listen to me!

(Lights down on the dining room, up on The Romans)

LONGINUS: You listen to me: I've no care for your points. But you would be wise to care for mine, for, while wet, it is sharp and bright, and filled with newfound vigor.

CABRAL: I always knew it, Longinus: there has always been a lazy hue in your eyes, waiting to be dyed with treachery.

QUINTUS: Quiet, Cabral! Quiet and I will not say it again! Longinus, what choice are you making?

LONGINUS: What choice can I make? I'm relegated to the will of the stars.

(Lights down on The Romans, up on the bedroom)

NICHOLAS: You think I don't know the stars? You two. You two, you think you're the only ones with a television? Who read the papers? I know it. I know it all. And you're not going?

(Lights up on the dining room)

TYCHO: Johannes, I'm going.

MICHAEL: *(Coming to consciousness)* Going where?

(Lights down on the bedroom)

TYCHO: My guess, were I to hazard one—and I've always understood the stars better than men—would be that my bladder has burst.

KEPLER: Your…what?

TYCHO: Jebb here thinks maybe I was poisoned, but that's my theory. There was a lot of drinking, Kepler. And it's impolite to leave the reveling, you know. Bathroom breaks. Not as much as never attending, as is your standard, but I care more for these things.

KEPLER: How long ago?

TYCHO: Maybe eleven.

KEPLER: Hours?

TYCHO: No, no…days.

KEPLER: Tycho…

TYCHO: Yes?

KEPLER: I didn't…we have to get you some physic.

TYCHO: Oh my, it's much too late for that.

JEBB: The dream, part three!

KEPLER: Not now, Jebb! So, what, Brahe; you're just content to die?

TYCHO: Content, resigned…I don't see much recourse.

(Lights down on the banquet, up on the bedroom)

NICHOLAS: We're running out of time.

IANTHE: Don't fall asleep, Michael.

NICHOLAS: She's right, Mike. You've probably got a concussion. You could die if you pass out.

MICHAEL: You wouldn't want that now, would you, you gun-toting suddenly-a-nutbag?

NICHOLAS: Well, I'm not sure yet, right? Isn't that the point? Pay attention, Mike. You're embarrassing yourself. I don't think you get a say in this anyway.

(Lights down on the bedroom, up on The Romans)

QUINTUS: Then who is to read the stars? To make the decision?

(Lights down on The Romans, up on the dining room)

TYCHO: The houses of the sky are guiding, but not determinative, I think.

(Lights down on the dining room, up on the bedroom)

MICHAEL: I don't give a shit what you think.

(Lights down on the bedroom, up on the banquet)

KEPLER: I agree.

TYCHO: No you don't.

(Lights down on the dining room, up on The Romans)

LONGINUS: Why should it matter?

QUINTUS: Rome needs soldiers.

LONGINUS: Rome needs street sweepers.

QUINTUS: Same thing!

CABRAL: Isn't that funny.

(Lights up on the bedroom)

MICHAEL: Nick, I love you and all, but man, if you don't kill me…

QUINTUS: One more peep out of you and…

MICHAEL & QUINTUS: I'm gonna kill you.

(Lights down on The Romans, up on the dining room)

IANTHE & KEPLER: Let's be reasonable.

TYCHO: Reasonable?

KEPLER: Nobody has to die here.

MICHAEL: Yeah right.

JEBB: This was a lot more fun in the beginning.

NICHOLAS: I'll say.

KEPLER: Just be quiet.

(Lights down on the dining room, up on The Romans)

LONGINUS: Maybe I'll become a monk.

IANTHE: Think this over.

CABRAL: Where's the fun in that?

NICHOLAS: Shhh… Here it comes.

(Lights fade on The Romans)

(IANTHE and MICHAEL stare at NICHOLAS. A moment passes.)

IANTHE: Nick…

NICHOLAS: Shhh! Be quiet.

(Lights fade on the bedroom. The stage sits in darkness for a moment.)

(A dog barks.)

KEPLER, NICHOLAS & QUINTUS: I said be quiet!

(The lights come up in all directions, bright and blinding. After a moment, they begin to fade, revealing all three playing areas. CABRAL lies prone. The characters all seem to get a look at each other. Lights fade out.)

END OF ACT ONE

ACT TWO

(The set is largely as it was: three playing areas, for the bedroom, Romans and banquet. Now, however, there is a light constantly present upstage, which cases the inactive players and locales in silhouette. Lights up on the dining room)

TYCHO: There it is.

KEPLER: Did you see them?

TYCHO: When first I saw the nova, I thought it was the birth of a star. One minute it wasn't there and the next it was. Or so it seemed… What do you think, Kepler?

KEPLER: What's that?

TYCHO: You don't agree with me on anything, but still…the nova: am I right?

KEPLER: Right how?

TYCHO: Is it birth, this flash? Because just now, I had this terrible feeling that perhaps death can be like a flash, too…and that for some, this flash might be the first notice we receive. Maybe, then, death too is birth, at least in this case. That death gives birth to tombstones, and that tombstones might more solidly stand for the dead than did the dead while living. *(Silence)* I'm sorry…did that get confusing at the end there?

KEPLER: No, Tycho. Not at all. Maybe a little, towards the end, but mostly not at all.

TYCHO: Good. I don't like it when things end without clarity.

(Lights down on the dining room, up on The Romans)

(CABRAL lies prone, probably dying. LONGINUS and QUINTUS stare at him.)

(After a moment:)

QUINTUS: There it is.

LONGINUS: Did you see them?

QUINTUS: You got your stars, and you got your sacrifice. To think you thought your days of murder were over. What a clean cut.

LONGINUS: I didn't…

QUINTUS: Who has the spear, Longinus?

CABRAL: Friends…

QUINTUS: Not now, Cabral. You've been flashing that thing about all day, looking for someone to cut it on.

LONGINUS: I already cut it on someone.

QUINTUS: I'll say you did.

(Lights down on The Romans, up on the bedroom)

NICHOLAS: There it is.

IANTHE: Did you see them?

NICHOLAS: *(As if in his own world)* Before, it all seemed so blurry. Or, not blurry…like everything was shaky. Like parallax. You know when you're moving and you look at everything and it's all moving with you, but slower. It's like it all wobbles. That's why a lot of people—smart people, I mean, like scientists—didn't believe the Earth went around The Sun. Back when they didn't. 'Cause if the Earth were moving, the stars should have wobbled. When…but they didn't. So we had to be standing still. Peaceful; central. But here's the…uh, thing; rub. Is that it is moving, we—we are moving. And the stars, they are wobbling. It's just that they're so far…farther than people ever thought possible. So the blurring is too small to see. Parallax. Just a failure of imagination.

MICHAEL: What are you talking about?

NICHOLAS: The ignorance routine is running flat, Mike.

IANTHE: Honestly, Nicholas, we don't know what you're talking about.

NICHOLAS: It's worse from you. I don't know how stupid he is, but I've got an idea how smart you are. And, besides all that, I heard you.

MICHAEL: Heard us what?

NICHOLAS: I don't think it was an accident. Now, I mean. At the time, I figured it was a coincidence—not what you were saying, but that I heard it. But, when I think about it now, it's like, well, duh, he let me…no: he made me hear you. I don't know. Maybe it's a test.

IANTHE: What test?

NICHOLAS: I don't know; this is all just coming to me. This part. You know, like a gradual realization.

(*Lights down on the bedroom, up on the dining room*)

TYCHO: It's unfair, Kepler, that we relegate epiphany to bursts. Why should it have to be sudden? Why can't epiphany be gradual?

KEPLER: Not to be contrary, but it's possible that the definition of epiphany is what rules that out.

TYCHO: I understand that, Kepler, but in my experience, that point at which all the information—all the knowledge—rushes forth, it takes some time for it to become clear. It needs to thin, to osmoses, for it to all make sense. As a suddenly well-lit room that blinds until the eyes acclimate. You understand?

KEPLER: Yes…

TYCHO: You have to wonder, you must have wondered for a while now, about my observations, yes? My charts?

KEPLER: Well, of course.

TYCHO: You came here, having heard that I had records and observations and papers of a breadth totally unrivaled by all others. And then you just sat around, waiting. Hoping I'd give them to you. Just wishing they'd fall into your lap. So, what I wonder is, which did you think about more: what might be contained within those notes, or how it is that this drunken buffoon could have amassed them?

KEPLER: It…depended on my mood. Mostly I thought about the papers at night, and when I couldn't sleep, due to noise or discomfort, I would…ruminate on your…antics. But when it was calm and I could lie in bed and glance out my window to the sky, I would imagine what sense there could be to it.

TYCHO: Sense to the sky?

KEPLER: Exactly.

TYCHO: That is it, isn't it? What we do. Try to put sense to the sky.

KEPLER: Find sense to the sky.

TYCHO: Hm. Well, that's the question. I'll tell you, when I was young and I looked at the stars, I saw magic. "What are these things?" I would wonder. And the planets! The planets, which then seemed different from stars just barely, just the difference in color and magnitude. But as I grew and watched I saw them move. Saw the planets move in a way that the stars did not. That was a slow epiphany…that things which seem so similar, marvelous things, could actually be entirely different.

KEPLER: But why so different, and in what way?

TYCHO: That was the question! And the same question for you and me. I followed Mars so intently. Years. Every night I would mark it, observe it. And then, finally, when I had it all down, I started on Venus… didn't even take a moment to breathe. But in the middle of my studies, I thought I had it figured out. Thought I could predict the whole thing. I looked up from my abacus and realized I could chart the rest without even looking. Just for a moment, that's what I thought. I dropped my guard. I had gone about my work with teeth-grating enthusiasm and intensity. So long as I kept up my drive, it seemed like I could go forever. But that one hesitation, that one lag…doomed me. I didn't know it at first, you see, but it did, it doomed me. I'm convinced. From there is all fizzled, like the weight of my scales had just flipped. It became more about what I had, and what I had done than what I might do. Gladly. I had lived well, and it was time to celebrate that. You see? It was the celebration: it just swallowed me whole.

KEPLER: You've led a happy life, Tycho.

TYCHO: So what? What good is happiness? I could've done more. Jebb!

JEBB: Yes, sire.

TYCHO: Bring the papers.

JEBB: Yes, sire. *(He exits.)*

TYCHO: That's all. That's all I wanted to say to you. I could've done more. I'm about to lose my legs, you know. I'm on my way out.

KEPLER: I know.

TYCHO: So I wanted you to know that I understand.

KEPLER: Understand what?

TYCHO: I understand why.

(JEBB *reenters with portfolios and scrolls:* TYCHO's *research.*)

TYCHO: Thank you, Jebb. Kepler, these are yours.

KEPLER: Your work?

TYCHO: It's what you're after, right? Jebb thinks you don't deserve it. That you haven't done anything, haven't made any sacrifice worthy. But I know that's not true. And I don't blame you for it. You're right: I could've done more.

(Lights down on the dining room, up on The Romans)

QUINTUS: It's unfair, what you've done here today, Longinus.

LONGINUS: Quintus, I've done nothing.

QUINTUS: Now you brandish your temper at me?

LONGINUS: We should get him some help.

CABRAL: I'm right here.

QUINTUS: The lament of the guilty.

LONGINUS: It's basic compassion!

QUINTUS: Cabral, Cabral: can you hear me? You were right. I thought perhaps he was just bellowing, but look; look what he's done to you.

LONGINUS: Quintus, it is painfully obvious that you are the one who felled him.

QUINTUS: With what, Longinus? Hm? Ask yourself that. I'd be inclined to believe you, if I weren't the unarmed friend of the boy. It's alright, you beautiful boy, I won't let him hurt you again.

LONGINUS: Again? He's dying!

QUINTUS: Don't gloat.

LONGINUS: What?!

QUINTUS: Cabral, please… tell us, who is it that has struck you?

LONGINUS: It doesn't even matter, let's just find someone to help…

QUINTUS: That's right: seek to impede upon the truth. Go ahead, Cabral.

CABRAL: Well, I don't really know. There was some arguing?

QUINTUS: That's right: he was arguing with us.

LONGINUS: Oh for the sake of…

CABRAL: And then I saw a flash.

LONGINUS: Oh yeah.

QUINTUS: Right. Boy, I'd almost forgotten about that.

LONGINUS: Seems like that would have been important enough to give some attention to.

QUINTUS: And yet…

LONGINUS: And yet we completely overlooked it.

QUINTUS: What can you do?

CABRAL: Brothers…

LONGINUS: It just seems strange that we would totally ignore something like that.

CABRAL: Things are getting dark.

QUINTUS: But we did.

CABRAL: Please help me.

QUINTUS: Completely ignored it.

LONGINUS: What does that say about us?

QUINTUS: Now, now. Don't be so harsh. I don't think one oversight should reflect too terribly upon our characters.

LONGINUS: It's just that I'd meant to be so observant.

QUINTUS: Even a tightly woven net lets water past.

LONGINUS: True. But what about a water bladder?

(LONGINUS *and* QUINTUS *look at each other a moment, then burst out laughing.*)

QUINTUS: Water bladders!

LONGINUS: Who's ever heard of such a thing?

QUINTUS: And imagine what it would take for a bladder to actually, physically burst!

LONGINUS: It's implausible!

QUINTUS: Ah, well, that's our Cabral... Oh, my: Cabral, I'd forgotten all about you.

CABRAL: Please...

QUINTUS: Yes, tell us who it was what stabbed you.

CABRAL: Why aren't you helping me?

QUINTUS: In a minute.

CABRAL: What?

QUINTUS: Just answer the question.

CABRAL: I don't know. I guess...I guess Longinus had the spear.

QUINTUS: See, Longinus: told you it was you.

LONGINUS: Really, Cabral? I honestly thought I hadn't.

QUINTUS: You heard it straight from the elk's mouth.

LONGINUS: It's just...what was my motivation?

QUINTUS: How should we know, you goof!

LONGINUS: You're right...I guess I could have done it.

QUINTUS: Buck up. I don't blame you for it. (*A moment*) How about you, Cabral?

(*Lights down on the Romans, up on the bedroom*)

NICHOLAS: Everything was so blurry. But it came to me. An epiphany. It's a stillness. And whether that stillness means I can be stationary, be central, or that I can just be too distant to feel the vibrations of this life, I don't know. But either way, it's truth. So what's the answer to the test? Is it supposed to be a "how far will I go" kind of thing, or, a…is it about forgiving? Or justice? Maybe, but that…I don't know. Justice doesn't sound right.

MICHAEL: I think it's about forgiveness. Don you, Ianthe?

NICHOLAS: *(Laughing)* Mikey, you're a riot, man, you know that? Look, we're running out of time here. I've got to go soon, and the question is, who's going with me. Maybe it's like the thieves on the cross, right? "Do not despair; one of the thieves was saved… *(He points the gun at* IANTHE*)* Do not presume; one of the thieves was damned." *(He points the gun at* MICHAEL*)* Last night. I heard you. I woke up and my bladder was full. I was going for the bathroom and I looked out the window and there was this…light. Like a star, but it didn't move like a star. I approached the window and…the most beautiful thing I've ever seen. And then, it talked to me.

MICHAEL: It what now?

NICHOLAS: It explained how, every once in a while, it opens up a portal in a star, to let the righteous out. And it said it would open up tonight. You see? It's heaven. And I stumbled back, because I suddenly felt I shouldn't be looking at it. I fell to the foot of your door and heard the two of you talking. One of Ianthe's poems.

IANTHE: Oh shit.

NICHOLAS: About going off to the stars together, just the two of you. And no. No. It came to me, not you. But should I show a little more compassion than you had planned for me? What do you think?

MICHAEL: Take me, then. I wasn't going to go anyway. Ianthe was. See? Look: the bag.

IANTHE: Give it up, Michael.

MICHAEL: What?

IANTHE: You're right, Nicholas. We were ready to leave. We were ready to leave and we weren't taking you with us.

NICHOLAS: No, no…see: I knew it.

IANTHE: So, no: I wouldn't show us that compassion. Because we weren't about to show it to you.

NICHOLAS: Wait, but…no, see, the test of it…

IANTHE: There's no test. No meaning to it.

NICHOLAS: But, the bag…

IANTHE: Those are separate things. Just coincidence they seem so similar.

NICHOLAS: Yeah, but, the odds of that?

IANTHE: I don't know, Nick. What the fuck am I, a statistician?

NICHOLAS: You could come. Just you, I mean. Leave him and come with me. If you were going…better to leave an angel than a traitor.

IANTHE: Wouldn't that make me both.

NICHOLAS: An angel can't be a traitor.

IANTHE: Than a traitor can't be…fuck it. Here's the long and short of it, Nick: I don't love you. I love Mike so much, and don't love you so much, that I'm not going to heaven. What do you think of that?

NICHOLAS: So be it. (*Placing the gun under his chin*)

MICHAEL: Wait, Nick.

NICHOLAS: You know, guys, I could probably look down on you, from where I'm going.

IANTHE: Nick…

NICHOLAS: And you; you might see me.

IANTHE: You'll be totally different. We wouldn't be able to tell you from the stars.

NICHOLAS: There might be some difference. In color or…magnitude.

MICHAEL: Nick, I don't think…

NICHOLAS: Let's find out.

(As NICHOLAS *fires the gun, the lights go down immediately on the bedroom and up on the dining room.)*

TYCHO: May I not seem to have lived in vain. *(He collapses.)*

KEPLER: Tycho? Tycho?

(A moment passes with no response. JEBB *crosses to* KEPLER *and places* TYCHO's *papers in front of him.)*

(KEPLER sits with the papers in front of him, but does not open them

KEPLER: What was the third part?

JEBB: You don't deserve it. Or these. But he thought you'd done something…

KEPLER: I did what I had to do.

JEBB: And that is?

KEPLER: Come on, Jebb: you're a smart little clairvoyant. You ever heard of a bursting bladder?

JEBB: It's only through his forgiveness that you…

KEPLER: What matters is how a man lives, not how he dies.

JEBB: I thought the whole point of this was the opposite.

KEPLER: …It's a little of both.

(Lights down on the dining room, up on The Romans)

QUINTUS: You're a murderer, Longinus. And you know what we do to murderers?

LONGINUS: You…

QUINTUS: We banish them.

LONGINUS: I don't know what to say…

QUINTUS: Go! I'll allow you your spear, for protection.

LONGINUS: May my new life bring me greater things.

QUINTUS: Sure, sure. Or at least less of the same.

(LONGINUS exits.)

(Lights down on The Romans, up on the bedroom)

(Immediately when the lights rise, NICHOLAS falls to the ground, dead.)

MICHAEL: Jesus Christ! We've got to help him.

IANTHE: Mike, he's dead.

MICHAEL: Fuck.

IANTHE: Well. It's not our fault. *(She begins unpacking her bag.)*

MICHAEL: But you…

IANTHE: I'm not happy about it, Mike. But…look: we all make choices. It's just that sometimes we: don't get a choice about what ones.

MICHAEL: So…he was just crazy, then?

IANTHE: Looks like it.

MICHAEL: But, that light. We saw it. There it is, right now.

IANTHE: I don't know, Mike, but obviously it's not… what? Heaven? Some weird alien god or…whatever. He was nuts. It's probably just a stupid nova.

MICHAEL: Still, he predicted it.

IANTHE: We don't know that. We don't know what he really thought, or knew, or when. Is there any sense to the mind?

MICHAEL: As much as there is to the sky.

(Lights down on the bedroom. Only the silhouettes of the remaining characters are intact. No other light comes up. The back light slowly dims until end.)

JEBB: The dream, part three!

CABRAL: The light is fading.

JEBB: In sudden darkness, he wandered aimlessly, with only a bottle of wine. He wondered what composed this veil.

QUINTUS: That's just night falling.

KEPLER: *(Now perusing* TYCHO's *papers)* I've never see the sky so clearly.

JEBB: And for that matter, where was he?

CABRAL: Where's Longinus?

QUINTUS: Gone now. He was crazy anyhow.

MICHAEL: What if he wasn't crazy?

IANTHE: He took a poem for a plot. He was pretty obviously crazy.

KEPLER: The orbits are parabolic! It's so obvious!

JEBB: Hoping his starting place was significant, he looked for a way to mark his path.

QUINTUS: He set down the path North, with that spear in hand.

KEPLER: We're revolving. Not central. No significance to our place.

JEBB: And so he began slowly pouring out his wine behind him as he walked, the smell giving him recall of his route. But as he did, he felt himself emptying.

CABRAL: It hurts. How sharp that blade.

QUINTUS: Counterclockwise swipes of the stone, starting at the hilt and moving outwards.

JEBB: When the last drop was poured out, he looked at his hand and saw that he could see right through it.

MICHAEL: You're not leaving.

IANTHE: You heard the deal: He gets to go, so we have to stay.

QUINTUS: He got a good end of the deal, at least.

JEBB: Panicked, he turned around and saw from the stain his wine had left, himself, standing more solid but less him. And then he just floated away, into the sky.

KEPLER: Nothing significant at all.

(The stage is now totally dark. There is a small twinkle of a star.)

END OF PLAY

www.ingramcontent.com/pod-product-compliance
Lightning Source LLC
Chambersburg PA
CBHW070034110426
42741CB00035B/2770